VOICES & POETRY OF
IRELAND

SOURCEBOOKS MEDIAFUSION™
AN IMPRINT OF SOURCEBOOKS, INC.®
NAPERVILLE, ILLINOIS

Copyright © 2003, 2005 by Folk Promotions, Ltd.
Cover and internal design © 2005 by Sourcebooks, Inc.
Cover photos © Getty Images
Internal photos © see page 103
Sourcebooks and the colophon are registered trademarks of Sourcebooks, Inc.

All rights reserved. No part of this book may be reproduced in any form or by any electronic or mechanical means including information storage and retrieval systems—except in the case of brief quotations embodied in critical articles or reviews—without permission in writing from its publisher, Sourcebooks, Inc.

For reprint permissions, please see page 101

Published by Sourcebooks, Inc.
P.O. Box 4410, Naperville, Illinois 60567-4410
(630) 961-3900
fax: (630) 961-2168
www.sourcebooks.com

Originally published in 2003 in the UK by HarperCollinsPublishers

Library of Congress Cataloging-in-Publication Data

Voices and poetry of Ireland.
    p. cm.
  Includes index.
  ISBN 1-4022-0404-3 (alk. paper)
  1. English poetry--Irish authors. 2. Ireland--Poetry.

PR8851.V65 2005
821.008'9417--dc22

                                        2004030651

Printed and bound in the United States of America
LB   10   9   8   7   6   5   4   3   2   1

CONTENTS

TRACK LIST

VOICES & POETRY OF IRELAND

AMERGIN
(Dates Unknown)

Amergin was a Milesian prince or druid who settled in Ireland hundreds of years before Christ and is from the *Leabhar Gabhala* or Book of Invasions. He is considered one of Ireland's earliest poets, and "The Mystery" is attributed as the first Irish poem.

READ BY

PATRICK BERGIN was born and raised in Dublin. He has appeared in myriad film and television productions, including *Robin Hood* and *Patriot Games*, and co-starred with Julia Roberts in the Hollywood hit film *Sleeping with the Enemy*.

The Mystery

Translated by Douglas Hyde

I am the wind which breathes upon the sea,
I am the wave of the ocean,
I am the murmur of the billows,
I am the ox of the seven combats,
I am the vulture upon the rocks,
I am a beam of the sun,
I am the fairest of plants,
I am a wild boar in valour,
I am a salmon in the water,
I am a lake in the plain,
I am a word of science,
I am the point of the lance of battle,
I am the God who created in the head the fire.

Who is it who throws light into the meeting on the mountain?
Who announces the ages of the moon?
Who teaches the place where couches the sun?
     (If not I)

ANONYMOUS
(Dates Unknown)

READ BY

MAEVE BINCHY was born in County Dublin and was educated at University College Dublin. Her first novel was published in 1982 and was an instant success. Since then, she has written more than a dozen novels and short story collections, each of them bestsellers. She is married to the writer and broadcaster Gordon Snell.

Pangur Bán

Translated by Robin Flower

I and Pangur Bán, my cat,
'Tis a like task we are at;
Hunting mice is his delight,
Hunting words I sit all night.

Better far than praise of men
'Tis to sit with book and pen;
Pangur bears me no ill will,
He too plies his simple skill.

'Tis a merry thing to see
At our tasks how glad are we,
When at home we sit and find
Entertainment to our mind.

Oftentimes a mouse will stray
In the hero Pangur's way;
Oftentimes my keen thought set
Takes a meaning in its net.

'Gainst the wall he sets his eye
Full and fierce and sharp and sly;
'Gainst the wall of knowledge I
All my little wisdom try.

When a mouse darts from its den,
O how glad is Pangur then!
O what gladness do I prove
When I solve the doubts I love!

So in peace our tasks we ply,
Pangur Bán, my cat and I;
In our hearts we find our bliss,
I have mine and he has his.

Practice every day has made
Pangur perfect in his trade;
I get wisdom day and night
Turning darkness into light.

WILLIAM ALLINGHAM
(1824–1889)

Born in Ballyshannon, County Donegal, Allingham was a frequent visitor to London as a young man where he became friendly with the poet Alfred Lord Tennyson. In 1850, he published his first volume of poetry, which was followed by several others including the long poem *Laurence Bloomfield in Ireland*, largely regarded as his most important work. He married in 1874 and published several more volumes of poetry before his death fifteen years later.

READ BY

MAUREEN POTTER has been described as the queen of Irish comedy, appearing in over 50 pantomimes at Dublin's Gaiety Theatre. She starred in her own summer show, *Gaels of Laughter*, for an unbroken run of 18 seasons and has appeared with such Irish theatrical luminaries as Michael MacLiammoir, Cyril Cusack and Siobhan McKenna.

THE FAIRIES

Up the airy mountain,
Down the rushy glen,
We daren't go a-hunting
For fear of little men;
Wee folk, good folk,
Trooping all together;
Green jacket, red cap,
And white owl's feather!

Down along the rocky shore
Some make their home —
They live on crispy pancakes
Of yellow tide-foam;
Some in the reeds
Of the black mountain lake,
With frogs for their watch-dogs,
All night awake.

High on the hill-top
The old King sits;
He is now so old and grey
He's nigh lost his wits.
With a bridge of white mist
Columbkill he crosses,
On his stately journeys
From Slieveleague to Rosses;
Or going up with music
On cold starry nights
To sup with the Queen
Of the gay Northern Lights.

They stole little Bridget
For seven years long;
When she came down again
Her friends were all gone.
They took her lightly back,
Between the night and morrow;
They thought that she was fast asleep,
But she was dead with sorrow.
They have kept her ever since
Deep within the lake,
On a bed of flag-leaves,
Watching till she wake.

By the craggy hill-side,
Through the mosses bare,
They have planted thorn-trees
For pleasure here and there.
Is any man so daring
As dig one up in spite,
He shall find their sharpest thorns
In his bed at night.

Up the airy mountain,
Down the rushy glen,
We daren't go a-hunting
For fear of little men;
Wee folk, good folk,
Trooping all together;
Green jacket, red cap,
And white owl's feather!

ARTHUR O'SHAUGHNESSY
(1844–1881)

O'Shaughnessy's working life, from 1861 to his death, was spent as an assistant in the British Museum. He was a friend of Rossetti and of Ford Madox Brown and married the sister of another poet, Philip Bourke Marston. French poetry was his prevailing influence and his volumes of poetry include *An Epic of Women*, *Lays of France*, and *Music and Moonlight*. His most enduring poem, known from its first line, "We are the music makers," was later set to music by Edward Elgar and Zoltán Kodály. O'Shaughnessy married Eleanor Marston in 1873, with whom he wrote *Toy–land*, a book of children's stories.

READ BY

RONNIE DREW is regarded as the quintessential voice of Dublin. Born in Dun Laoghaire in 1934, he sprang to international fame as a member of the legendary Dubliners and continues to play to audiences worldwide.

ODE

We are the music-makers,
And we are the dreamers of dreams,
Wandering by lone sea-breakers,
And sitting by desolate streams;
World-losers and world-forsakers,
On whom the pale moon gleams:
Yet we are the movers and shakers
Of the world for ever, it seems.

With wonderful deathless ditties
We build up the world's great cities,
And out of a fabulous story
We fashion an empire's glory:
One man with a dream, at pleasure,
Shall go forth and conquer a crown;
And three with a new song's measure
Can trample an empire down.

We, in the ages lying
In the buried past of the earth,
Built Nineveh with our sighing,
And Babel itself with our mirth;
And o'erthrew them with prophesying
To the old of the new world's worth;
For each age is a dream that is dying,
Or one that is coming to birth.

OSCAR WILDE
(1854–1900)

Having attended Trinity College Dublin and Oxford University, where he excelled in his studies and won prizes for his poetry, Wilde moved to London where he published his first volume of poetry in 1881. On a trip to the United States, he met fellow poets Walt Whitman and Henry Longfellow, and returned to London to write poems, plays, and his first and only novel, *The Picture of Dorian Gray*. His notably successful plays include *Lady Windermere's Fan* and *The Importance of Being Earnest*, which earned him critical and commercial success. In 1895, Wilde was arrested because of his relationship with Lord Alfred Douglas and was sentenced to two years' imprisonment. His long poem *The Ballad of Reading Gaol* is an account of his experiences in prison. He died of meningitis three years after his release.

READ BY

GAVIN FRIDAY was born in Dublin in 1959. He is a singer, composer, performer and painter. He is the founding member of the legendary avant-garde punk group The Virgin Prunes.

from The Ballad of Reading Gaol

...He did not wear his scarlet coat,
For blood and wine are red,
And blood and wine were on his hands
When they found him with the dead,
The poor dead woman whom he loved,
And murdered in her bed.

He walked amongst the Trial Men
In a suit of shabby grey;
A cricket cap was on his head,
And his step seemed light and gay;
But I never saw a man who looked
So wistfully at the day.

I never saw a man who looked
With such a wistful eye
Upon that little tent of blue
Which prisoners call the sky,
And at every drifting cloud that went
With sails of silver by.

I walked with other souls in pain,
Within another ring,
And was wondering if the man had done
A great or little thing,
When a voice behind me whispered low,
"That fellow's got to swing."

Dear Christ! the very prison walls
Suddenly seemed to reel,
And the sky above my head became
Like a casque of scorching steel;
And, though I was a soul in pain,
My pain I could not feel.

I only knew what hunted thought
Quickened his step, and why
He looked upon the garish day
With such a wistful eye;
The man had killed the thing he loved,
And so he had to die.

Yet each man kills the thing he loves,
By each let this be heard,
Some do it with a bitter look,
Some with a flattering word,
The coward does it with a kiss,
The brave man with a sword!

Some kill their love when they are young,
And some when they are old;
Some strangle with the hands of Lust,
Some with the hands of Gold:
The kindest use a knife, because
The dead so soon grow cold.

Some love too little, some too long,
Some sell, and others buy;
Some do the deed with many tears,
And some without a sigh:
For each man kills the thing he loves,
Yet each man does not die.

OSCAR WILDE

READ BY

GABRIEL BYRNE was born in Dublin. His acting career began at Dublin's Focus Theatre and he has since starred in over 35 films, including *The Usual Suspects*, *Stigmata*, and *End of Days*. He resides in New York.

To L.L.

Could we dig up this long-buried treasure,
Were it worth the pleasure,
We never could learn love's song,
We are parted too long.

Could the passionate past that is fled
Call back its dead,
Could we live it all over again,
Were it worth the pain!

I remember we used to meet
By an ivied seat,
And you warbled each pretty word
With the air of a bird;

And your voice had a quaver in it,
Just like a linnet,
And shook, as the blackbird's throat
With its last big note;

And your eyes, they were green and grey
Like an April day,
But lit into amethyst
When I stooped and kissed;

And your mouth, it would never smile
For a long, long while,
Then it rippled all over with laughter
Five minutes after.

You were always afraid of a shower,
Just like a flower:
I remember you started and ran
When the rain began.

I remember I never could catch you,
For no one could match you,
You had wonderful, luminous, fleet
Little wings to your feet.

I remember your hair – did I tie it?
For it always ran riot –
Like a tangled sunbeam of gold:
These things are old.

I remember so well the room,
And the lilac bloom
That beat at the dripping pane
In the warm June rain;

And the colour of your gown,
It was amber-brown,
And two yellow satin bows
From your shoulders rose.

And the handkerchief of French lace
Which you held to your face –
Had a small tear left a stain?
Or was it the rain?

On your hand as it waved adieu
There were veins of blue;
In your voice as it said good-bye
Was a petulant cry,

"You have only wasted your life."
          (Ah, that was the knife!)
When I rushed through the garden gate
It was all too late.

Could we live it over again,
Were it worth the pain,
Could the passionate past that is fled
Call back its dead!

Well, if my heart must break,
Dear love, for your sake,
It will break in music, I know,
Poets' hearts break so.

But strange that I was not told
That the brain can hold
In a tiny ivory cell,
God's heaven and hell.

❀

W B Yeats
(1865–1939)

Born in Dublin, Yeats was educated there and in London. The young Yeats was very much part of the fin de siècle in London, but at the same time he was active in societies that attempted an Irish literary revival. His first volume of verse appeared in 1887, but in his earlier period his dramatic production outweighed his poetry both in bulk and in import. Together with Lady Gregory he founded the Irish Theatre, which was to become the Abbey Theatre, and served as its chief playwright until the movement was joined by J M Synge. His plays include *The Countess Cathleen*, *The Land of Heart's Desire*, *Cathleen ni Houlihan*, *The King's Threshold*, and *Deirdre*. He was appointed to the Irish Senate in 1922 and he also received the Nobel Prize, chiefly for his dramatic works. His poetry includes the volumes *The Wild Swans at Coole*, *Michael Robartes and the Dancer*, *The Tower*, *The Winding Stair and Other Poems*, and *Last Poems and Plays*.

READ BY

Born in 1928 in County Wexford, **ANTHONY CRONIN** is a poet, novelist, critic and biographer. His novels include *Life of Riley* and *Identity Papers*. He has also published a biography of Flann O'Brien, *No Laughing Matter*, and a major biography of Samuel Beckett, *The Last Modernist*.

THE FISHERMAN

Although I can see him still,
The freckled man who goes
To a grey place on a hill
In grey Connemara clothes
At dawn to cast his flies,
It's long since I began
To call up to the eyes
This wise and simple man.
All day I'd looked in the face
What I had hoped 'twould be
To write for my own race
And the reality;
The living men that I hate,
The dead man that I loved,
The craven man in his seat,
The insolent unreproved,
And no knave brought to book
Who has won a drunken cheer,
The witty man and his joke
Aimed at the commonest ear,
The clever man who cries

The catch-cries of the clown,
The beating down of the wise
And great Art beaten down.
Maybe a twelvemonth since
Suddenly I began,
In scorn of this audience,
Imagining a man
And his sun-freckled face,
And grey Connemara cloth,
Climbing up to a place
Where stone is dark under froth,
And the down turn of his wrist
When the flies drop in the stream:
A man who does not exist,
A man who is but a dream;
And cried, "Before I am old
I shall have written him one
Poem maybe as cold
And passionate as the dawn."

W B YEATS

READ BY

LIAM CLANCY is a founding member of the Clancy Brothers and Tommy Makem group. He was a resident actor at Harvard's Poet Theater in 1957–58; in 1960 he co-produced Yeats's plays at New York's Poetry Center. He received an honorary doctorate from the University of Limerick in 2002, the same year that his first volume of memoirs, *The Mountain of the Women*, was published.

THE SECOND COMING

Turning and turning in the widening gyre
The falcon cannot hear the falconer;
Things fall apart; the centre cannot hold;
Mere anarchy is loosed upon the world,
The blood-dimmed tide is loosed, and everywhere
The ceremony of innocence is drowned;
The best lack all convictions, while the worst
Are full of passionate intensity.

Surely some revelation is at hand;
Surely the Second Coming is at hand.
The Second Coming! Hardly are those words out
When a vast image of Spiritus Mundi
Troubles my sight: somewhere in the sands of the desert
A shape with lion body and the head of a man,
A gaze blank and pitiless as the sun,
Is moving its slow thighs, while all about it
Reel shadows of the indignant desert birds.
The darkness drops again; but now I know
That twenty centuries of stony sleep
Were vexed to nightmare by a rocking cradle,
And what rough beast, its hour come round at last,
Slouches towards Bethlehem to be born?

W B YEATS

READ BY

MILO O'SHEA began his acting career as a child in Dublin. He continued his career at the Gate and Abbey theatres before moving on to London's West End and Broadway. He has starred in numerous films, including *Barbarella*, *The Verdict*, and *The Butcher Boy*, and TV shows such as *Cheers* and *Frasier*. He recently completed the films *Puck-oon* and *Mystics*.

THE BALLAD OF FATHER GILLIGAN

The old priest Peter Gilligan
Was weary night and day;
For half his flock were in their beds
Or under green sods lay.

Once, while he nodded on a chair,
At the moth-hour of eve,
Another poor man sent for him,
And he began to grieve.

"I have no rest, nor joy, nor peace,
For people die and die";
And after cried he, "God forgive!
My body spake, not I!"

He knelt, and leaning on the chair
He prayed and fell asleep;
And the moth-hour went from the fields,
And stars began to peep.

They slowly into millions grew,
And leaves shook in the wind;
And God covered the world with shade,
And whispered to mankind.

Upon the time of sparrow-chirp
When the moths came once more,
The old priest Peter Gilligan
Stood upright on the floor.

"Mavrone, mavrone! The man has died
While I slept on the chair";
He roused his horse out of its sleep
And rode with little care.

He rode now as he never rode,
By rocky lane and fen;
The sick man's wife opened the door:
"Father! You come again!"

"And is the poor man dead?" he cried.
"He died an hour ago."
The old priest Peter Gilligan
In grief swayed to and fro.

"When you were gone, he turned and died
As merry as a bird."
The old priest Peter Gilligan
He knelt him at that word.

"He Who hath made the night of stars
For souls who tire and bleed,
Sent one of His great angels down
To help me in my need.

He Who is wrapped in purple robes,
With planets in His care,
Had pity on the least of things
Asleep upon a chair."

W B YEATS

ANDREA CORR is the lead singer of The Corrs. She has appeared in the films *The Commitments*, *Evita*, and *The Boys from County Clare*.

NEVER GIVE ALL THE HEART

Never give all the heart, for love
Will hardly seem worth thinking of
To passionate women if it seem
Certain, and they never dream
That it fades out from kiss to kiss;
For everything that's lovely is
But a brief, dreamy, kind delight.
O never give the heart outright,
For they, for all smooth lips can say,
Have given their hearts up to the play.
And who could play it well enough
If deaf and dumb and blind with love?
He that made this knows all the cost,
For he gave all his heart and lost.

W B Yeats

READ BY

SEAMUS HEANEY was born in 1939 in County Derry and lives in Dublin. *Death of a Naturalist*, his first volume of poetry, was published in 1966 and since then he has become one of the leading poets of his generation. He was Professor of Poetry at Oxford University from 1989 to 1994 and in 1995 he was awarded the Nobel Prize.

WHAT THEN?

His chosen comrades thought at school
He must grow a famous man;
He thought the same and lived by rule,
All his twenties crammed with toil;
"What then?" sang Plato's ghost. "What then?"

Everything he wrote was read,
After certain years he won
Sufficient money for his need,
Friends that have been friends indeed;
"What then?" sang Plato's ghost. "What then?"

All his happier dreams came true –
A small old house, wife, daughter, son,
Grounds where plum and cabbage grew,
Poets and Wits about him drew;
"What then?" sang Plato's ghost. "What then?"

"The work is done," grown old he thought,
"According to my boyish plan;
Let the fools rage, I swerved in naught,
Something to perfection brought";
But louder sang that ghost, "What then?"

WINIFRED M LETTS
(1882–1972)

Born in County Wexford, Letts later moved to Kent. Her poems include *Songs from Leinster* and she was one of the few female poets to wrote about the effects of World War I. She also wrote plays and novels, including *Christina's Son*, *The Eyes of the Blind*, *The Challenge*, *More Songs*, *Hallowe'en*, and *Poems of the War*.

READ BY

CIARAN MacMATHUNA joined RTE in 1954 with special responsibility for Irish traditional music and song on radio. He is best known for RTE's most enduring radio show *Mo Cheol Thu*, the Sunday morning bilingual program of music, song, and poetry that has been running for over 30 years.

TO A MAY BABY

To come at tulip time how wise!
Perhaps you will not now regret
The shining gardens, jewel set,
Of your first home in Paradise
Nor fret
Because you may not quite forget.

To come at swallow-time how wise!
When every bird has built a nest;
Now you may fold your wings and rest
And watch this new world with surprise;
A guest
For whom the earth has donned her best.

To come when life is gay how wise!
With lambs and every happy thing
That frisks on foot or sports on wing,
With daisies and with butterflies,
But Spring
Had nought so sweet as you to bring.

F R Higgins
(1896–1941)

Born in County Mayo, Higgins was influenced by the Irish Literary Revival and became a close friend of both W B Yeats and Austin Clarke. He contributed reviews to the *Irish Statesman* and poetry to *The Dial*, *Spectator*, *Atlantic Monthly*, and *Dublin Magazine*. He was also Director of the Abbey Theatre for a period and founding member and secretary of the Irish Academy of Letters. He published five volumes of poetry in his lifetime.

READ BY

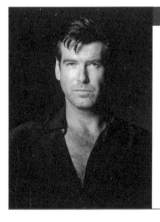

PIERCE BROSNAN is best known for his role as the current James Bond. His work includes films such as *Dante's Peak* and *The Thomas Crown Affair*, as well as the Bond movies *Goldeneye*, *Tomorrow Never Dies*, *The World Is Not Enough*, and *Die Another Day*. Originally from County Meath, he now lives in California with his family.

FATHER AND SON

Only last week, walking the hushed fields
Of our most lovely Meath, now thinned by November,
I came to where the road from Laracor leads
To the Boyne river - that seemed more lake than river,
Stretched in uneasy light and stript of reeds.

And walking longside an old weir
Of my people's, where nothing stirs — only the shadowed
Leaden flight of a heron up the lean air —
I went unmanly with grief, knowing how my father,
Happy though captive in years, walked last with me there.

Yes, happy in Meath with me for a day
He walked, taking stock of herds hid in their own breathing;
And naming colts, gusty as wind, once steered by his hand,
Lightnings winked in the eyes that were half shy in greeting
Old friends — the wild blades, when he gallivanted the land.
For that proud, wayward man now my heart breaks —
Breaks for that man whose mind was a secret eyrie,
Whose kind hand was sole signet of his race,
Who curbed me, scorned my green ways, yet increasingly loved me
Till Death drew its grey blind down his face.

And yet I am pleased that even my reckless ways
Are living shades of his rich calms and passions —
Witnesses for him and for those faint namesakes
With whom now he is one, under yew branches,
Yes, one in a graven silence no bird breaks.

LOUIS MACNEICE
(1907–1963)

Born in Belfast and brought up in Carrickfergus, County Antrim, MacNeice studied Classics and Philosophy at Oxford and both of these subjects informed his poetry. He was reknowned as a translator, literary critic, playwright, auto-biographer, BBC producer and feature writer as well as poet. His major works are *The Dark Tower*, *Roundabout Way* (written as Louis Malone), *Blind Fireworks*, *Poems*, *The Earth Compels*, *Autumn Journal*, *Plant and Phantom*, *Springboard*, *Holes in the Sky*, *Ten Burnt Offerings*, *Autumn Sequel*, *Visitations*, *Solstices*, *The Burning Perch*, and *Persons from Porlock*.

READ BY

JOHN LYNCH first gained notice in 1984 with his portrayal of a terrorist who falls for an older woman in Pat O'Connor's film *Cal*. He played a leading role in *In the Name of the Father* and has starred in such films as *Sliding Doors*, *Some Mother's Son*, and *Evelyn*.

THE SUNLIGHT ON THE GARDEN

The sunlight on the garden
Hardens and grows cold,
We cannot cage the minute
Within its nets of gold,
When all is told
We cannot beg for pardon.

Our freedom as free lances
Advances towards its end;
The earth compels, upon it
Sonnets and birds descend;
And soon, my friend,
We shall have no time for dances.

The sky was good for flying
Defying the church bells
And every evil iron
Siren and what it tells;
The earth compels,
We are dying, Egypt, dying

And not expecting pardon,
Hardened in heart anew,
But glad to have sat under
Thunder and rain with you,
And grateful too
For sunlight on the garden.

LOUIS MACNEICE

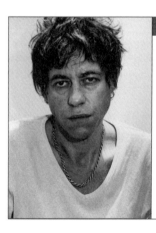

READ BY

BOB GELDOF is known in many guises: pop star, poet, politician and media mogul. Bob Geldof was the lead singer of the Boomtown Rats, but is best known as the man behind Live Aid, which raised over a hundred million dollars worldwide for the famine in Ethiopia. In 1986 Geldof received an honorary knighthood for his charity efforts.

BAGPIPE MUSIC

It's no go the merrygoround, it's no go the rickshaw,
All we want is a limousine and a ticket for the peepshow.
Their knickers are made of crêpe-de-chine, their shoes are
made of python,
Their halls are lined with tiger rugs and their walls with heads
of bison.

John MacDonald found a corpse, put it under the sofa,
Waited till it came to life, and hit it with a poker,
Sold its eyes for souvenirs, sold its blood for whisky,
Kept its bones for dumb-bells to use when he was fifty.

It's no go the Yogi-Man, it's no go Blavatsky,
All we want is a bank balance and a bit of skirt in a taxi.

Annie MacDougall went to milk, caught her foot in the heather,
Woke to hear a dance record playing of Old Vienna.
It's no go your maidenheads, it's no go your culture,
All we want is a Dunlop tyre and the devil mend the puncture.

The Laird o' Phelps spent Hogmanay declaring he was sober,
Counted his feet to prove the fact and found he had one foot over.
Mrs Carmichael had her fifth, looked at the job with
repulsion,
Said to the midwife, "Take it away; I'm through with over-production."

It's no go the gossip column, it's no go the ceilidh,
All we want is a mother's help and a sugar-stick for the baby.

Willie Murray cut his thumb, couldn't count the damage,
Took the hide of an Ayrshire cow and used it for a bandage.
His brother caught three hundred cran when the seas were lavish,
Threw the bleeders back in the sea and went upon the parish.

It's no go the Herring Board, it's no go the Bible,
All we want is a packet of fags when our hands are idle.

It's no go the picture palace, it's no go the stadium,
It's no go the country cot with a pot of pink geraniums,
It's no go the Government grants, it's no go the elections,
Sit on your arse for fifty years and hang your hat on a pension.

It's no go my honey love, it's no go my poppet,
Work your hands from day to day, the winds will blow the profit.
The glass is falling hour by hour, the glass will fall for ever,
But if you break the bloody glass you won't hold up the weather.

MÁIRTÍN Ó DÍREÁIN
(1910–1988)

Born on the Aran Islands, Ó Díreáin worked as a civil servant for much of his life. His main works include the poetry collections *Rogha Dánta*, *Ó Mórna agus Dánta Eile*, *Ar Ré Dhearóil*, *Cloch Choirnéil*, *Crainn is Cairde*, *Ceacht an Éin*, *Dánta 1939-79*, *Béasa an Túir*, *Tacar Dánta/Selected Poems*, and *Craobhóg: Dán*. His autobiographical essays are collected as *Feamainn Bhealtine*. His awards include the An Chomhairle Ealaíon/The Arts Council Awards, the Butler Prize (with Eoghan Ó Tuairisc) and the Ossian Prize for Poetry.

READ BY

MICK LALLY appeared on Irish TV screens every Sunday night for 22 years in the soap opera *Glenroe*. He was involved with the founding of Galway's world-renowned Druid theatre company in 1975 and has appeared in many of its productions.

ÓMÓS DO JOHN MILLINGTON SYNGE/ HOMAGE TO JOHN MILLINGTON SYNGE

An toisc a thug tú chun mo dhaoine	The impulse that brought you to my people
Ón gcein mheith don charraig gharbh	From the distant pasture to the harsh rock
Ba cheile lei an chré bheo	Was partnered by the living clay
Is an leid a scéith as léan is danaid.	And the intimations of loss and sorrow.
Nior eistis scéal na gcloch,	You didn't listen to the tale of the stones,
Bhi eacht i scéal an teallaigh,	Greatness lived in the tale of the hearth,
Nior speis leat leac na cill,	You paid no heed to tombstone or graveyard,
Ni thig éamh as an gcré mharbh.	No whimper escapes the lifeless dust.
Do dhuinigh Deirdre romhat sa ród	Deirdre appeared before you on the road
Is curach Naoise do chas Ceann Gainimh,	And Naoise's currach weathered Ceann Gainimh;
D'imigh Deirdre is Naoise leo	Deirdre and Naoise went to their death
Is chaith Peigin le Seáinin aithis.	And Pegeen flung abuse at Shawneen.
An leabhar ba ghnáth i do dhóid	The book was always in your hand
As ar chuiris breithe ar marthain;	You brought the words in it to life;
Ghabh Deirdre, Naoise is Peigin cló	Deirdre, Naoise and Pegeen took form
Is thug léim ghaisce de na leathanaigh.	And leaped like heroes from the pages.
Tá cleacht mo dhaoine ag meath,	The ways of my people decay,
Ni cabhair feasta an tonn mar fhalla,	The sea no longer serves as a wall,
Ach go dtaga Coill Chuain go hInis Meáin	But till Coill Chuain comes to Inis Meáin
Beidh na bréithre a chnuasais trath	The words you gathered then
Ar marthain fós i dteanga eachtrann.	Will live on in an alien tongue.

SEAMUS KAVANAGH

READ BY

BRENDA FRICKER was born in Dublin in 1945. In 1989 she won a Best Supporting Actress Oscar for her role in *My Left Foot*. She now works in films, television and theatre in Ireland, Great Britain, and the United States.

BIDDY MULLIGAN, THE PRIDE OF THE COOMBE

I'm a buxom fine widow, I live in a spot,
In Dublin they call it the Coombe;
My shops and my stalls are laid out on the street,
And my palace consists of one room.
I sell apples and oranges, nuts and split peas,
Bananas and sugar-stick sweet,
On Saturday night I sell secondhand clothes
From the floor of my stall on the street.

You may travel from Clare
To the County Kildare,
From Francis Street on to Macroom,
But where would you see
A fine widow like me?
Biddy Mulligan, the pride of the Coombe.

I sell fish on a Friday, spread out on a board
The finest you'd find in the sae,
But the best is my herrings, fine Dublin Bay herrings,
There's herrings for dinner today.
I have a son Mick, and he's great on the flute
He plays in the Longford Street Band,
It would do your heart good to see him march out,
On a Sunday for Dollymount strand.

You may travel from Clare
To the County Kildare,
From Francis Street on to Macroom,
But where would you see
A fine widow like me?
Biddy Mulligan, the pride of the Coombe.

In the Park on a Sunday, I make quite a dash,
The neighbours look on with surprise,
With my Aberdeen shawlie thrown over my head,
I dazzle the sight of their eyes.
At Patrick Street corner for sixty-four years,
I've stood and no one can deny,
That while I stood there, no person could dare
To say black was the white of my eye.

You may travel from Clare
To the County Kildare,
From Francis Street on to Macroom,
But where would you see
A fine widow like me?
Biddy Mulligan, the pride of the Coombe.

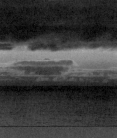

DONAGH MACDONAGH
(1912–1968)

Born in Dublin, MacDonagh practiced law, serving on the bench in County Wexford for many years and as a judge in Dublin up to his death. He was also a broadcaster, poet and playwright, publishing *Twenty Poems* with Niall Sheridan and staging the first Irish production of *Murder in the Cathedral*. His ballad opera, *Happy as Larry*, was the most successful play in London in post-war years.

READ BY

Born and raised in Castleknock, Dublin, **COLIN FARRELL** has become a major Hollywood actor. A string of movie appearances include *Alexander*, *Tigerland*, *Phone Booth*, *The Recruit*, *American Outlaws*, and *Ordinary Decent Criminal*. Colin is a graduate of Dublin's Gaiety School of Drama.

DUBLIN MADE ME

Dublin made me and no little town
With the country closing in on its streets
The cattle walking proudly on its pavements
The jobbers, the gombeenmen and the cheats

Devouring the fair-day between them
A public-house to half a hundred men
And the teacher, the solicitor and the bank-clerk
In the hotel bar drinking for ten.

Dublin made me, not the secret poteen still
The raw and hungry hills of the West
The lean road flung over profitless bog
Where only a snipe could nest.

Where the sea takes its tithe of every boat.
Bawneen and currach have no allegiance of mine,
Nor the cute self-deceiving talkers of the South
Who look to the East for a sign.

The soft and dreary midlands with their tame canals
Wallow between sea and sea, remote from adventure,
And Northward a far and fortified province
Crouches under the lash of arid censure.

I disclaim all fertile meadows, all tilled land
The evil that grows from it and the good,
But the Dublin of old statutes, this arrogant city,
Stirs proudly and secretly in my blood.

Sigerson Clifford
(1913–1984)

Although born in Cork, Clifford was regarded as a native of Cahersiveen, where his family relocated. His father was a tailor in Top Street, Cahersiveen, the location of his famous song, "The Boys of Barr na Sráide." He recorded the main events of his life in verse, later collected in *Ballads of a Bogman*.

READ BY

Born in Dingle in Co. Kerry, **MICHEAL Ó MUIRCHEARTAIGH** is the quintessential voice of the GAA. His radio commentary, delivered in the unmistakable accent of a Gaelgeoir, is beloved throughout Ireland, and his witticisms are quoted from pub stool to internet site.

THE BOYS OF BARR NA SRÁIDE

O the town it climbs the mountain and looks upon the sea,
And sleeping time or waking 'tis there I long to be,
To walk again that kindly street, the place I grew a man
And the Boys of Barr na Sráide went hunting for the wran.

With cudgels stout we roamed about to hunt the droileen
We looked for birds in every furze from Letter to Dooneen:
We sang for joy beneath the sky, life held no print or plan
And we Boys in Barr na Sráide, hunting for the wran.

And when the hills were bleeding and the rifles were aflame,
To the rebel homes of Kerry the Saxon stranger came,
But the men who dared the Auxies and beat the Black and Tans
Were the Boys of Barr na Sráide hunting for the wran.

And here's a toast to them tonight, the lads who laughed with me,
By the groves of Carhan river or the slopes of Beenatee,
John Dawley and Batt Andy, and the Sheehans Con and Dan,
And the Boys of Barr na Sráide who hunted for the wran.

And now they toil on foreign soil, where they have gone their way
Deep in the heart of London town or over on Broadway.
And I am left to sing their deeds, and praise them while I can
Those Boys of Barr na Sráide who hunted for the wran.

And when the wheel of life runs down and peace comes over me,
O lay me down in that old town between the hills and sea,
I'll take my sleep in those green fields the place my life began,
Where the Boys of Barr na Sráide went hunting for the wran.

PATRICK GALVIN
(1927–)

Born in Cork, Galvin's poetry collections include *Heart of Grace*, *Christ in London*, *The Wood-burners*, *Man on the Porch*, *Madwoman of Cork*, and *Folktales for the General*. His plays include *And Him Stretched*, *Cry the Believers*, *Nightfall to Belfast*, *The Last Burning*, *We Do It for Love*, *The Devil's Own People*, and *My Silver Bird*. His radio plays include *City Child Come Tailing Home*, *Wolfe*, *Class of '39*, and *Quartet for Nightown*. He has published two separate volumes of autobiography: *Song for a Poor Boy* and *Song for a Raggy Boy*. The third part, *Song for a Fly Boy*, is published with the first two as *The Raggy Boy Trilogy*. *Song for a Raggy Boy* has been made into a film starring Aidan Quinn.

READ BY

ARDAL O'HANLON is one of Ireland's most acclaimed comedians. His role as Father Dougal McGuire in Channel 4's *Father Ted* won him the BAFTA for Best Comedy Actor in 1999. His most recent incarnation is that of novelist, with his first book, *The Talk of the Town*, a bestseller.

PLAISIR D'AMOUR

Spring
My father
Against the victories of age
Would not concede defeat
He dyed his hair
And when my mother called
He said he wasn't there.

My mother, too
Fought back against the years
But in her Sunday prayers
Apologised to God.
My father said there was no God
"And that one knows it to her painted toes."

My mother smiled.
She'd plucked her eyebrows too
And wore a see-through skirt
With matching vest.
"He likes French knickers best" she said
"I'll have them blest."

My father raged.
He liked his women young, he said
And not half-dead.
He bought a second-hand guitar he couldn't play
And sang the only song he knew –
Plaisir d'Amour

Summer
When summer came
My father left the house
He tied a ribbon in his hair
And wore a Kaftan dress.
My mother watched him walking down the street
"He'll break his neck in that," she said –
"As if I care."

He toured the world
And met a guru in Tibet.
"I've slept with women too" he wrote
"And they not half my age."
My mother threw his letter in the fire –
"The lying ghett – he couldn't climb the stairs
With all his years."

She burned her bra
And wrote with lipstick on a card –
"I've got two sailors in the house
From Martinique.
They've got your children's eyes."
My father didn't wait to answer that
He came back home.

And sitting by the fire
He said he'd lied
He'd never slept with anyone but her.
My mother said she'd never lied herself –
She'd thrown the sailors out an hour before he came.
My father's heart would never be the same –
Plaisir d'Amour

Autumn
Through autumn days
My father felt the leaves
Burning in the corners of his mind.
My mother, who was younger by a year,
Looked young and fair.
The sailors from the port of Martinique
Had kissed her cheek.

He searched the house
And hidden in a trunk beneath the bed
My father found his second-hand guitar.
He found her see-through skirt
With matching vest.
"You wore French knickers once" he said
"I liked them best."

"I gave them all away," my mother cried
"To sailors and to captains of the sea.
I'm not half-dead
I'm fit for any bed – including yours."
She wore a sailor's cap
And danced around the room
While father strummed his second-hand guitar.

He made the bed
He wore his Kaftan dress
A ribbon in his hair.
"I'll play it one more time," he said
"And you can sing."
She sang the only song they knew –
Plaisir d'Amour

Winter
At sixty-four
My mother died
At sixty-five
My father.

Comment from a neighbour
Who was there;
"They'd pass for twenty."
Plaisir d'Amour

LELAND BARDWELL
(1928–)

Born in India of Irish parents, Bardwell was brought to Ireland at the age of two. Her collections of poetry are *The Mad Cyclist*, *The Fly and the Bedbug*, *Dostoevsky's Grave*, *New and Selected Poems*, and *The White Beach, New & Selected Poems 1960–1988*. Her novels are *Girl on a Bicycle*, *That London Winter*, *The House*, *There We Have Been*, and *Mother to a Stranger*. Her plays include *Thursday* and *Open–Ended Prescription*. She has also broadcast radio plays, including *The Revenge of Constance* and *Just Another Killing*. Her musical, *Edith Piaf*, also toured Ireland. She lives in County Sligo.

READ BY

Since she was first published in 1995, **MARIAN KEYES** has become a publishing phenomenon. Her six novels— *Watermelon*, *Lucy Sullivan is Getting Married*, *Rachel's Holiday*, *Last Chance Saloon*, *Sushi for Beginners*, and *Angels*—are all international bestsellers, having sold over seven million copies.

THEMS YOUR MAMMY'S PILLS

They'd scraped the top soil off the garden
and every step or two they'd hurled a concrete block
bolsters of mud like hippos from the hills
rolled on the planters plantings of the riff-raff of the city.

The schizophrenic planners had finished off their job
folded their papers, put away their pens –
the city clearances were well ahead.

And all day long a single child was crying
while his father shouted: Don't touch them,
Thems your mammy's pills.

I set to work with zeal to play "Doll's House,"
"Doll's life," "Doll's Garden"
while my adolescent sons played Temporary Heat
in the living room out front
and drowned the opera of admonitions:
Don't touch them, thems your mammy's pills.

Fragile as needles the women wander forth
laddered with kids, the unborn one ahead
to forge the mile through mud and rut
where mulish earth-removers rest, a crazy sculpture.

They are going back to the city for the day
this is all they live for –
going back to the city for the day.

The line of shops and solitary pub
are camouflaged like check points on the border
the supermarket stretches emptily
a circus of sausages and time
the till-girl gossips in the veg department

Once in a while a woman might come in
to put another pound on
the electronic toy for Christmas.

From behind the curtains every night
the video lights are flickering, butcher blue
Don't touch them, thems your mammy's pills.

No one has a job in Killinarden
nowadays they say it is a no go area
I wonder, then, who goes and does not go
in this strange forgotten world
of video and valium

I visited my one time neighbour
not so long ago. She was sitting
in the hangover position
I knew she didn't want to see me
although she'd cried when we were leaving

I went my way
through the quietly rusting motor cars and prams
past the barricades of wire, the harmony of junk.
The babies that I knew are punk-size now
and soon children will have children
and new voices ring the *leit motif*:

Don't touch them, thems your mammy's pills.

for Edward McLachlan

JOHN MONTAGUE
(1929–)

Born in Brooklyn, New York, but reared on the family farm in County Tyrone, Montague's poetry includes *Forms of Exile, Poisoned Lands, A Chosen Light, Tides; The Rough Field, A Slow Dance, The Great Cloak, The Dead Kingdom, Mount Eagle, The Love Poems, Time in Armagh, Collected Poems,* and *Smashing the Piano*. His fiction includes *The Lost Notebook* and the short stories *An Occasion of Sin*. He has edited *Bitter Harvest*, an anthology of Irish poetry. Among numerous prizes and honors, he has received the American Ireland Fund Literary Award. He lives in County Cork.

READ BY

PADDY MOLONEY is the founder and leader of The Chieftains. In the forty years since he founded the group, they have played across the world, and won a panoply of awards, including six Grammys, an Emmy, and an Oscar.

THE COUNTRY FIDDLER

My uncle played the fiddle – more elegantly the violin –
A favourite at barn and crossroads dance,
He knew "The Morning Star" and "O'Neill's Lament."

Bachelor head of a house full of sisters,
Runner of poor racehorses, spendthrift,
He left for the New World in an old disgrace.

He left his fiddle in the rafters
When he sailed, never played afterwards,
A rural art stilled in the discord of Brooklyn.

A heavily-built man, tranquil-eyed as an ox,
He ran a wild speakeasy, and died of it.
During the Depression many dossed in his cellar.

I attended his funeral in the Church of the Redemption,
Then, unexpected successor, reversed time
To return where he had been born.

During my schooldays the fiddle rusted
(The bridge fell away, the catgut snapped)
Reduced to a plaything, stinking of stale rosin.

The country people asked if I also had music
(All the family had had) but the fiddle was in pieces
And the rafters remade, before I discovered my craft.

Twenty years afterwards, I saw the church again,
And promised to remember my burly godfather
And his rural craft after this fashion:

So succession passes, through strangest hands.

RICHARD HARRIS

(1930–2002)

Richard Harris was born in Limerick in 1930. He became a Hollywood super-
star and his many memorable performances range from *The Sporting Life* in 1963
to *Gladiator* in 2000.

READ BY

As famous for his off-screen antics as his acting, **RICHARD HARRIS** also loved literature and poetry; he reads his own poem here. Harris died in October 2002.

CHRISTY BROWN CAME TO TOWN

Christy Brown came to town riding on a wheelchair

Christy Brown came to town riding on a wheelchair
Back strapped to wheel and chair
Freewheeling down all his days
Into the byways in our heads
Visions bursting from his pen
Ink in blood, left foot in rapture
Riding through Fleet Street pulp
Past paper stand and paste
Ploughing stairs to heaven
Riding on and on and on
His chariot wheels
Conquering heroes in space
In the time allotted for his spin.
Reared in masses his childhood
Playpen on concrete slabs
Turned into flowing fountains
In his fountain pen toes
Ceasing to suffer in the kennel of his bark
Spent dark years with his ears
Tied to his mother's tongue.
Where are you mother?
I am here, I am here Christy
Growing flowers in your yard
Sending fruit to the marketplace in your soul
Patiently bending my breasts
To feed the hunger in your mind.
Dear bended lady
Drawing she drew in midnight whispers
The elements of verse
Vocalising grammar, building his armory for battle
Filling his long, sleepless, limping nights
With the music of her challenge
And she took a dead season from her womb
And built a birth as bright as Christmas.

In his schoolroom slum
That buried some and crippled most
The toast from her womb grew legs in her words
And walked long distance to the corners of the earth
Striding beyond Getsemane past the Avenue of the Sorrows
Out of Golgatha into resurrection.

Christy Brown came to town riding on a donkey

Christy Brown came to town riding on a donkey
Streets in palms carpeting his Sunday visit
He rode barebacked the donkey of the Apocalypse
Over bridges where crippled water stood still
In the lame shores of our crime.
He rode heaven high over tears and pity
Through the attending city
Where skeletons hid high in the cupboards of our complacency
He rode on and on and on and on he rode
On the laughter in his size
Everlasting in song
Storming our ears in wonder
Making his face shine upon us
And throwing from the seaweeds of his wisdom
Iodine
To heal the wounds of a waiting world.

GERRY CORR
(1933–)

Born in Dundalk, County Louth, Corr's great interests are music and literature. In his poetry, opposites are kin as he blends tragedy and humor in a unique but necessary vision of life. He is the father of the family pop group The Corrs.

READ BY

SHARON CORR plays violin in The Corrs. The Corrs have sold 30 million records and have won awards globally, together with two Grammy nominations for their *In Blue* album. Sharon reads her father's poem.

FIRST ANNUAL REPORT

A year on, my love,
A year since we parted,
You to the prayer-wrapped unknown,
Me to a cell called freedom

In your place I have memory,
A stingy usurper
Dispensing crumbs
From the banquet of your table

Like a donkey in Omeath
Kicking my pride
And your laughter
Animating the Mournes

Or champagne Saturday
When we whooped and danced
To new celestial arrivals
On our cherished firmament,

Your light is on dim now, my love,
Yet blinding flashes of you
Startle me awake
From the barren limbo of dreams,

You'll be pleased God is back.
He left when you died.
Went a.w.o.l.
Like He'd been found out
Not having the answers
And permitting instead a soothing indulgence:
Why hast Thou forsaken me

Yet there again, my dear,
I must allow for pre-occupation
With glamorous new arrival,
Introductions all round,
Glasses raised and all that,
Yours a spritzer, my love?

That's about it for now, my dear,
Except to say the blubbering is ceased
And sorrow's sickly syrup of self
Expunged from the menu

Well...in hope and in prayer, that is,

My love

BRENDAN KENNELLY
(1936–)

Kennelly achieved international recognition with his poem "Cromwell," following this with the even more notorious *Book of Judas*, which topped the Irish bestsellers list. He has published over 20 other volumes of poetry as well as four verse plays, two novels and a substantial body of criticism. He is a renowned editor and anthologist, and is Professor of Modern Literature at Trinity College, Dublin.

READ BY

BONO is the lead singer of U2. U2 released their first album in 1980 and have since sold over 100 million albums worldwide, winning 14 Grammys and six Brit Awards along the way. Bono lives in Dublin with his wife and four children.

GOD'S LAUGHTER

Someone had mercy on language
changed it into something else I can touch
I can touch
        grow to love, murmured Ace
as he heard the stranger talking of how
laughter comes from God.

Who, hearing words from his own mouth
and from others, can stop himself
laughing or freezing in terror

at sound bubbling up out of infinite
emptiness? Well, fill it with pride
and let vanity strut along for the ride.

When the ride peters out at the edge
of small daring, that other sound
opens.

        This is the sound of God's laughter,
like nothing on earth, it fills
earth from grave to mountain-top,
lingers there a while, then like a great
bird spreading its wings for home or somewhere
like home,
        heads out into silence,
gentle and endless, longing to understand

children, killers of children, killers. Mercy. Silence. Sound.
Mercy. Sound. Word. Sound. Change, there must be
change. There is. Say flesh. Say love. Say dust.
Say laughter. Who will call the fled bird back?
Stand. Kneel. Curse. Pray. Give us this day
our daily laughter. Let it show the way.
Thank God someone has mercy
on the words we find we must say.

BRENDAN KENNELLY

READ BY

DANIEL O'DONNELL is one of Ireland's most popular exports. Hailing from Donegal, he has surpassed sales of five million albums and 1.5 million videos and his sell-out concert appearances have taken him from New York's Carnegie Hall to Sydney's Opera House.

POEM FROM A THREE YEAR OLD

And will the flowers die?

And will the people die?
And every day do you grow old, do I
grow old, no I'm not old, do
flowers grow old?

Old things – do you throw them out?

Do you throw old people out?

And how you know a flower that's old?

The petals fall, the petals fall from flowers,
and do the petals fall from people too,
every day more petals fall until the
floor where I would like to play I
want to play is covered with old
flowers and people all the same
together lying there with petals fallen
on the dirty floor I want to play
the floor you come and sweep
with the huge broom.

The dirt you sweep, what happens that,
what happens all the dirt you sweep
from flowers and people, what
happens all the dirt? Is all the
dirt what's left of flowers and
people, all the dirt there in a
heap under the huge broom that
sweeps everything away?

Why you work so hard, why brush
and sweep to make a heap of dirt?
And who will bring new flowers?
And who will bring new people? Who will
bring new flowers to put in water
where no petals fall on to the
floor where I would like to
play? Who will bring new flowers
that will not hang their heads
like tired old people wanting sleep?
Who will bring new flowers that
do not split and shrivel every
day? And if we have new flowers,
will we have new people too to
keep the flowers alive and give
them water?

And will the new young flowers die?

And will the new young people die?

And why?

SEAMUS HEANEY
(1939–)

Born in Derry, Heaney's bibliography is vast, his work encompassing poetry, criticism, theatre and translation. His major poetry collections are *Death of a Naturalist, Door Into the Dark, Wintering Out, North, Field Work, Selected Poems, 1965–1975, Poems, 1965–1975, Station Island, The Haw Lantern, New Selected Poems, 1966–1987, Seeing Things, The Spirit Level, The School Bag, Electric Light*, and *Finders Keepers*. Along with Ted Hughes, he edited *The Rattle Bag*. His translation of *Beowulf* won him the Whitbread Book of the Year in 1999 and he was awarded the Nobel Prize for Literature in 1995. He is a former Professor of Poetry at Oxford University and currently Ralph Waldo Emerson Poet-in-Residence at Harvard.

READ BY

SIR JAMES GALWAY was born in Belfast. He is regarded as both a supreme interpreter of the classical flute repertoire and a consummate entertainer. Through his extensive touring, over fifty best-selling RCA Victor albums, and his frequent television appearances, Sir James has endeared himself to millions worldwide.

THE RAIN STICK

Up-end the rain stick and what happens next
Is a music that you never would have known
To listen for. In a cactus stalk

Downpour, sluice-rush, spillage and backwash
Come flowing through. You stand there like a pipe
Being played by water, you shake it again lightly

And diminuendo runs through all its scales
Like a gutter stopping trickling. And now here comes
A sprinkle of drops out of the freshened leaves,

Then subtle little wets off grass and daisies;
Then glitter-drizzle, almost-breaths of air.
Up-end the stick again. What happens next

Is undiminished for having happened once,
Twice, ten, a thousand times before.
Who cares if all the music that transpires

Is the fall of grit or dry seeds through a cactus?
You are like a rich man entering heaven
Through the ear of a raindrop. Listen now again.

for Beth and Rand

SEAMUS HEANEY

READ BY

TOMMY MAKEM has written hundreds of songs, many of which have become standards in the repertoire of folk singers around the world. During the 13 years Tommy performed with The Clancy Brothers, they brought Irish music to the attention of audiences worldwide.

REQUIEM FOR THE CROPPIES

The pockets of our greatcoats full of barley –
No kitchens on the run, no striking camp –
We moved quick and sudden in our own country.
The priest lay behind ditches with the tramp.
A people, hardly marching – on the hike –
We found new tactics happening each day:
We'd cut through reins and rider with the pike
And stampede cattle into infantry,
Then retreat through hedges where cavalry must be thrown.
Until, on Vinegar Hill, the fatal conclave.
Terraced thousands died, shaking scythes at cannon.
The hillside blushed, soaked in our broken wave.
They buried us without shroud or coffin
And in August the barley grew up out of the grave.

MICHAEL LONGLEY
(1939–)

Born in Belfast, where he still lives, Longley was Writer Fellow at Trinity College Dublin in 1993. His works of poetry include *No Continuing*, *An Exploded View*, *Man Lying on a Wall*, *The Echo Gate*, *Poems 1963–1983*, *Poems 1963–1980*, *Gorse Fires*, for which he was awarded the 1991 Whitbread Prize for Poetry, *The Ghost Orchid*, *Broken Dishes*; *Selected Poems*, and *The Weather in Japan*, for which he received the 2001 Irish Times Irish Literature Prize for Poetry. His most recent collection, *The Weather in Japan*, won both the Hawthornden Prize and the T. S. Eliot Prize. He was awarded the Queen's Gold Medal for Poetry in 2001 and is also a Fellow of the Royal Society of Literature. He lives in Belfast with his wife, the critic Edna Longley.

READ BY

FERGAL KEANE is the son of actor Eamon Keane and the nephew of playwright John B Keane. He has been a Special Correspondent for BBC news for over ten years and has won many awards for his reporting. In 1996, Fergal was awarded an OBE.

ALL OF THESE PEOPLE

Who was it who suggested that the opposite of war
Is not so much peace as civilisation? He knew
Our assassinated Catholic greengrocer who died
At Christmas in the arms of our Methodist minister,
And our ice-cream man whose continuing requiem
Is the twenty-one flavours children have by heart.
Our cobbler mends shoes for everybody; our butcher
Blends into his best sausages leeks, garlic, honey;
Our cornershop sells everything from bread to kindling.
Who can bring peace to people who are not civilised?
All of these people, alive or dead, are civilised.

DEREK MAHON
(1941–)

Mahon's poetry collections include *Night–Crossing*, *The Snow Party*, *Poems 1962–1978*, *Courtyards in Delft*, *The Hunt By Night*, *Antarctica*, *The Yaddo Letter*, *The Yellow Book*, *The Hudson Letter*, and *Collected Poems*. His translations include *The Chimeras*, *High Time*, *The Selected Poems of Philippe Jaccottet*, *The Bacchae* of Euripedes, and Racine's *Phaedre*. His screenplays include *Summer Lightning* and his prose is collected as *Journalism*. His honors include the Irish American Foundation Award, a Lannan Foundation Award, a Guggenheim Fellowship, the Irish Times/Aer Lingus Poetry Prize, the American Ireland Fund Literary Award, the C.K. Scott Moncreiff Translation Prize, and the Eric Gregory Award. He was born in Belfast and currently lives in Dublin.

READ BY

PAT KENNY presents the morning radio program *Today with Pat Kenny* and hosts the Friday night television show *The Late Late Show*. He has also worked as a presenter of mainstream current affairs programs.

ANTARCTICA

"I am just going outside and may be some time."
The others nod, pretending not to know.
At the heart of the ridiculous, the sublime.

He leaves them reading and begins to climb,
Goading his ghost into the howling snow;
He is just going outside and may be some time.

The tent recedes beneath its crust of rime
And frostbite is replaced by vertigo:
At the heart of the ridiculous, the sublime.

Need we consider it some sort of crime,
This numb self-sacrifice of the weakest? No,
He is just going outside and may be some time –

In fact, for ever. Solitary enzyme,
Though the night yield no glimmer there will glow,
At the heart of the ridiculous, the sublime.

He takes leave of the earthly pantomime
Quietly, knowing it is time to go.
"I am just going outside and may be some time."
At the heart of the ridiculous, the sublime.

for Richard Ryan

DEREK MAHON

READ BY

NIALL TOIBIN has been in show business since 1948, performing in theatre, variety, cabaret, radio, TV and film. He starred in the Tony award-winning production of Brendan Behan's *Borstal Boy*, and is a familiar face on British and Irish TV from series such as *Bracken*, *The Irish RM*, and *Minder*.

EVERYTHING IS GOING TO BE ALL RIGHT

How should I not be glad to contemplate
the clouds clearing beyond the dormer window
and a high tide reflected on the ceiling?
There will be dying, there will be dying,
but there is no need to go into that.
The poems flow from the hand unbidden
and the hidden source is the watchful heart.
The sun rises in spite of everything
and the far cities are beautiful and bright.
I lie here in a riot of sunlight
watching the day break and the clouds flying.
Everything is going to be all right.

Eiléan Ní Chuilleanán
(1942–)

Born in Cork, ní Chuilleanán has published eight collections of poetry: *Acts and Monuments*, *Site of Ambush*, *Cork*, *The Second Voyage*, *The Rose Geranium*, *The Magdalene Sermon*, *The Brazen Serpent*, and *The Girl Who Married the Reindeer*. She won the Patrick Kavanagh Award for *Acts and Monuments* in 1973, and *The Magdalene Sermon* was shortlisted for the Irish Times-Aer Lingus Award in 1990 and nominated for the European Literature Prize in 1992. The Irish-American Cultural Institute awarded her the O'Shaughnessy Prize for Poetry in 1992. She lives in Dublin.

READ BY

Soccer star **NIALL QUINN** recently retired after a career both in the Premiership for Arsenal and Manchester City and at international level for Ireland. He was awarded an honorary MBE in recognition of his donation of the proceeds of his testimonial match to children's charities. He lives in County Kildare.

SWINEHERD

When all this is over, said the swineherd,
I mean to retire, where
Nobody will have heard about my special skills
And conversation is mainly about the weather.

I intend to learn how to make coffee, at least as well
As the Portuguese lay-sister in the kitchen
And polish the brass fenders every day.
I want to lie awake at night
Listening to cream crawling to the top of the jug
And the water lying soft in the cistern.

I want to see an orchard where the trees grow in straight lines
And the yellow fox finds shelter between the navy-blue trunks,
Where it gets dark early in summer
And the apple-blossom is allowed to wither on the bough.

EAVAN BOLAND
(1944–)

Born in Dublin, where she still lives, Boland has published several collections of poetry including *The War Horse*, *In Her Own Image*, *Night Feed*, *The Journey*, *Selected Poems*, *Outside History*, *An Origin Like Water—Collected Poems 1967–1987*, and *The Lost Land*. Her recent collections are *A Lost Land* and *Code*. A collection of prose writings, *Object Lessons*, was published in 1995, and with Mark Strand she has edited *The Making of a Poem* and *A Norton Anthology of Poetic Forms*.

READ BY

MARIAN FINUCANE was born in Dublin and educated at Scoil Chaitriona and the DIT School of Architecture. She joined RTE in 1974 as an announcer and currently presents the *Marian Finucane Show* on morning radio. Over the course of her career she has been honored with broadcasting awards including Entertainer of the Year Award and Woman of the Year Award.

NIGHT FEED

This is dawn
Believe me
This is your season, little daughter.
The moment daisies open,
The hour mercurial rainwater
Makes a mirror for sparrows.
It's time we drowned our sorrows.

I tiptoe in.
I lift you up
Wriggling
In your rosy, zipped sleeper.
Yes, this is the hour
For the early bird and me
When finder is keeper.

I crook the bottle.
How you suckle!
This is the best I can be,
Housewife
To this nursery
Where you hold on,
Dear life.

A silt of milk.
The last suck
And now your eyes are open,
Birth-coloured and offended.
Earth wakes.
You go back to sleep.
The feed is ended.

Worms turn.
Stars go in.
Even the moon is losing face.
Poplars stilt for dawn
And we begin
The long fall from grace.
I tuck you in.

MICHAEL HARTNETT

(1944–1999)

Born in County Limerick, Hartnett lived in Dublin for many years. His collections include *Anatomy of a Cliché, The Old Hag of Beare, Tao, Gypsy Ballads, A Farewell to English, Prisoners, Adharca Broic, An Phurgóid, Do Nuala: Foighne Chrainn, Inchichore Haiku, Ó Bruadair, Selected Poems of Dáibhí Ó Bruadair, A Necklace of Wrens, Poems to Younger Women, Dánta Naomh Eoin na Croise, The Killing of Dreams, Haicéad,* and *Ó Rathaille The Poems of Aodhaghán Ó Rathaille.* He translated the *Selected Poems of Nuala Ní Dhomhnaill,* co-wrote a play, *An Lasair Choille,* with Caitlín Maude and was co-editor, with James Liddy and Liam O'Connor, of *Arena* and, with Desmond Egan, of *Choice.* He was also poetry editor of the *Irish Times* and a recipient of an American Fund Literary Award.

READ BY

THEO DORGAN is a poet, editor, documentary scriptwriter and broadcaster. Born in Cork in 1953, he has published a number of collections of poetry *including The Ordinary House of Love, Rosa Mundi,* and *Sappho's Daughter.* He lives in Baldoyle in North Dublin.

DEATH OF AN IRISHWOMAN

Ignorant, in the sense
she ate monotonous food
and thought the world was flat,
and pagan, in the sense
she knew the things that moved
at night were neither dogs nor cats
but púcas and darkfaced men,
she nevertheless had fierce pride.
But sentenced in the end
to eat thin diminishing porridge
in a stone-cold kitchen
she clenched her brittle hands
around a world
she could not understand.
I loved her from the day she died.
She was a summer dance at the crossroads.
She was a card game where a nose was broken.
She was a song that nobody sings.
She was a house ransacked by soldiers.
She was a language seldom spoken.
She was a child's purse, full of useless things.

DAVID QUIN
(1950–)

Born in Dublin's Rotunda, Quin wrote the first thesis (as far as is known) on Seamus Heaney and has worked as a journalist with *Hibernia Review, Sunday Tribune* and the *Irish Independent*. He is now course leader of the MA in Journalism at the Dublin Institute of Technology. He won second prize in the OZ Whitehead Play Competition in 2001. "Pity the Islanders" won the National Poetry Prize of Ireland in 1992.

READ BY

Dublin musician and singer **DANNY DOYLE** was one of the leading voices in the Irish folk song revival of the 1960s. His number one hits include *Step it Out Mary, The Mucky Kid, Whiskey on a Sunday*, and *The Rare Ould Times*. He now resides in Virginia.

Pity the Islanders, Lucht an Oileáin

For they dwelt on a rock in the sea and not in a shining metropolis
and lived off the pick of the strand, the hunt of the hill, the fish in the sea
the wool off the sheep, and packets full of dollars; for they ate black pudding,

drank sleadaí squeezed from seaweed, treated themselves on Good Fridays
to tit-bits from the shore, and thought a man rich if he possessed two cows;
for they stuffed their pillows with puffins' feathers, and the sea roared

in their right ear and the north wind moaned in their left; for they were full
of sunlight and mist, wind and stone, rain and rock, but the Atlantic ocean
would not pay them a regular salary; and they did not fret about tumble driers

or grouse about the menu, for the wind would not let them strut, the
rain made them meek and the waves kept them low; for they feared vain-glory
and the evil eye, chewed bits of seaweed and prayed to the mother of God;

for their enemies were bailiffs, big fat trawlers, mainland shopkeepers
and crows after hens; for they made nothing fit for museum or art gallery
and uttered proverbs that came up from Cro Magnon man; for they lived

before Descartes, Newton, Freud, de Sade and Marx, invented no novel machine
or vice, and never discovered the multiple orgasm; for they lacked ambition,
built into the earth not the sky, and did not rob and plunder or scatter

corpses in their wake; for they lived before the age of trivia
and never made it to the age of anxiety, and did not suffer ennui because
there was turf to be cut; for they did not rush into the future,

leaving their hearts behind them, because they had no future.
Praise the islanders, lucht an Oileáin, for they were a fair people
who pelted the stranger with blessings and the bailiffs with volleys of stones;

for they were a gentle people, who twisted puffins' necks, patted babies' heads
and split the skulls of seals; for they were like the children of one mother with twenty
steps between each house; for they were quiet people, who never

stopped talking, full of malice and affection, whose delights were tea
and tobacco, a big ship on the waves, a donkey on the loose, a battle
of tongues, a boatful of rabbits, a dance, a story, a song in the dead of night;

for they were as mournful as wet sheep and as bright as gan nets;
were pagans who trusted in God, rubbed seal oil on their wounds,
welcomed wrecks but prayed for the corpses, and loved to fill their bellies

with the breeze that flows from the west; for they broke their backs with loads of fish
    and sand, turf and lobsters, and leant on walls to bask in the sun;
for their stage was not the city, nation or world, but the village, the island and the
neighbouring parishes, which are about the right size for a human being.

When they strolled beneath the Milky Way their laughter did not pollute the
night, for they kept their boats high on the waves and their roofs low to the ground
and were grateful for seals when God withheld pigs.

❁

PAUL MULDOON
(1951–)

Born in Portadown in County Armagh, Muldoon read English at Queen's University Belfast. While he was at university, Faber published his first collection of poems, *New Weather*. For several years he was a radio producer for BBC Northern Ireland. He moved to the U.S. in 1987 and has held various university teaching posts, most recently Director of the Creative Writing Program at Princeton University, where he is the Howard G. B. Clark Professor in the Humanities. In 1999 he was elected Professor of Poetry at Oxford University. He has won many awards and prizes, including the Geoffrey Faber Memorial Prize in 1991, the T S Eliot Award, the American Academy of Arts and Letters Award for Literature in 1996, and the Irish Times Irish Literature Prize.

READ BY

BILL WHELAN, Grammy award-winning composer of *Riverdance: The Show*, has worked extensively in theatre, television and film. His work in international film includes *Lamb*, which he co-composed with Van Morrison; his score for the Jim Sheridan/Terry George film *Some Mother's Son*; and the original score for the adaptation of Brian Friel's *Dancing at Lughnasa*, which starred Meryl Streep.

ANSEO

When the Master was calling the roll
At the primary school in Collegelands,
You were meant to call back *Anseo*
And raise your hand
As your name occurred.
Anseo, meaning here, here and now,
All present and correct,
Was the first word of Irish I spoke.
The last name on the ledger
Belonged to Joseph Mary Plunkett Ward
And was followed, as often as not,
By silence, knowing looks,
A nod and a wink, the Master's droll
"And where's our little Ward-of-court?"

I remember the first time he came back
The Master had sent him out
Along the hedges
To weigh up for himself and cut
A stick with which he would be beaten.
After a while, nothing was spoken;
He would arrive as a matter of course
With an ash-plant, a salley-rod.
Or, finally, the hazel-wand
He had whittled down to a whip-lash,
Its twist of red and yellow lacquers
Sanded and polished,
And altogether so delicately wrought
That he had engraved his initials on it.

I last met Joseph Mary Plunkett Ward
In a pub just over the Irish border.
He was living in the open,
In a secret camp
On the other side of the mountain.
He was fighting for Ireland,
Making things happen.
And he told me, Joe Ward,
Of how he had risen through the ranks
To Quartermaster, Commandant:
How every morning at parade
His volunteers would call back *Anseo*
And raise their hands
As their names occurred.

GERRY DAWE
(1952–)

Born in Belfast, Dawe is a lecturer at University College Galway and Trinity College Dublin. His poetry includes *Sheltering Places*, *The Lundys Letter*, and *Lake Geneva*, and he has also edited *The Younger Irish Poets* and *Across the Roaring Hill: The Protestant Imagination in Modern Ireland*. His criticism includes *How's the Poetry Going*, *False Faces*, and *Against Piety: Essays in Irish Poetry*.

READ BY

VAN MORRISON'S musical career spans more than four decades. He has produced over 20 studio albums and gained iconic status in Ireland and internationally with albums such as *Astral Weeks* and *Poetic Champions Compose*.

SOLSTICE

You arrived that bad winter
when I was like a man
walking in a circle no one else was near.

The lakes behind had frozen,
from the dump gulls came and went
and the news was all discontent,

of *Sell-out* and blame for the dead
country-boy faces that already were
fading from church wall and gate,

but the seas tightened their grip
when you faced the light and let rip
a first cry of bewilderment

at this beginning, the snow
buttressed against brilliant windows,
and where they washed you clean

I saw the ice outside fall
and imagined the fires burning
on the Hill of Tara ring

across the concealed earth
towards a silent hospital
and our standing still

all around you, Olwen,
transfixed by your birth
in such a bitter season.

for my daughter

Dennis O'Driscoll
(1954–)

Born in Thurles in County Tipperary, O'Driscoll is a former editor of *Poetry Ireland Review*, and one of Ireland's most widely published and respected critics of poetry. He has published several collections: *Kist*, *Hidden Extras*, *Long Story Short*, *The Bottom Line*, *Quality Time*, *Weather Permitting*, which was a London Poetry Book Society Recommendation and for which he was awarded the Lannan Poetry Prize, and *Exemplary Damages*. A selection from his *Pickings and Cuttings* column of poetry quotations, *As The Poet Said*, was published by Poetry Ireland in 1997. His prose writing is collected as *Troubled Thoughts, Majestic Dreams: Selected Prose Writings*. He lives in County Kildare.

READ BY

Joe Duffy presents RTE's *Liveline*, a popular phone-in show. Born in 1956, Joe started out as a producer and later became a reporter on *The Gay Byrne Show*. This led to him presenting several programs, including the media program *Soundbyte*.

SOMEONE

someone is dressing up for death today, a change of skirt or tie
eating a final feast of buttered sliced pan, tea
scarcely having noticed the erection that was his last
shaving his face to marble for the icy laying out
spraying with deodorant her coarse armpit grass
someone today is leaving home on business
saluting, terminally, the neighbours who will join in the cortege
someone is trimming his nails for the last time, a precious moment
someone's thighs will not be streaked with elastic in the future
someone is putting out milkbottles for a day that will not come
someone's fresh breath is about to be taken clean away
someone is writing a cheque that will be marked "drawer deceased"
someone is circling posthumous dates on a calendar
someone is listening to an irrelevant weather forecast
someone is making rash promises to friends
someone's coffin is being sanded, laminated, shined
who feels this morning quite as well as ever
someone if asked would find nothing remarkable in today's date
perfume and goodbyes her final will and testament
someone today is seeing the world for the last time
as innocently as he had seen it first

PETER SIRR
(1960–)

Born in Waterford, Sirr won the Patrick Kavanagh Award in 1982 and the poetry prize at Listowel Writers' Week the following year. His collections of poetry are *Marginal Zones*, *Talk, Talk*, *Ways of Falling*, *The Ledger of Fruitful Exchange*, and *Bring Everything*. He is director of the Irish Writers' Centre and lives in Dublin.

READ BY

JIM SHERIDAN began his career in Dublin theatre and went on to co-found the alternative Project Arts group. He headed to America where he shot to fame with his Oscar-nominated directorial debut *My Left Foot* which he also wrote. This was to form a successful partnership with the actor Daniel Day Lewis that went on to yield such films as *In the Name of the Father* and *The Boxer*. His 2002 film *In America* was nominated for three Golden Globes; Sheridan himself was nominated for writing the screenplay.

PETER STREET

I'd grown almost to love this street
each time I passed looking up
to pin my father's face to a window, feel myself

held in his gaze. Today there's a building site
where the hospital stood and I stop and stare
stupidly at the empty air, looking for him.

I'd almost pray some ache remain
like a flaw in the structure, something unappeasable
waiting in the fabric, between floors, in some

obstinate, secret room. A crane moves
delicately in the sky, in its own language.
Forget all that, I think as I pass, make it

a marvellous house; music should roam the corridors,
joy readily occur, St Valentine's
stubborn heart comes floating from Whitefriar Street

to prevail, to undo injury, to lift my father from his bed,
let him climb down the dull red brick, effortlessly,
and run off with his life in his hands.

PAUL WILLIAMS

READ BY

SINEAD O'CONNOR was catapulted to fame with the success of *Nothing Compares to U*, written by Prince. Since then Sinead's uncompromising stances on a variety of issues have placed her at the center of media and public debate.

PRIDE

They called him a "Molly," his family
Every day
Every week
Every year.
And still they were shocked when he told them
Your son
Your brother
Is queer.
As if he had committed a murder
Or a crime that they just couldn't bear
When he walked into their local pub
They walked out
Leaving him there.

He stood in a room full of strangers
His new boyfriend by his side
Emotionally numbed for an instant
He reached in and regained his pride.
A new pride emerged
One that carries today
When they run away from reality
He is proud to be gay.

RORY GLEESON
(1990–)

Rory is the youngest of the poets featured in this collection. His father, Brendan, reads his poem "Emotions," which he wrote for his English class.

READ BY

BRENDAN GLEESON is a former teacher who spent the 1990s earning increasing acclaim for his acting, most notably in *The General* in 1998. He also appears in the films *Braveheart*, *Cold Mountain*, *Gangs of New York*, and *28 Days Later*. He lives in Dublin.

EMOTIONS

I am a volcano, ready to erupt,
I am a three year old child at a Shakespeare play,
I am a caged bird, kept away from the world,
I am a squirrel in a field of nuts,
I am a child, at his first day of school,
I am a dog, trying to learn algebra,
I am all these emotions bundled in one , but most importantly
I am a person trying to finish this poem
Before the teacher kills me.

INDEX OF FIRST LINES

PRINT PERMISSIONS

The publishers would like to acknowledge the following for permission to reproduce copyright material. Every effort has been made to trace the copyright holders of the material contained in this book but in some instances this has not proved to be possible. In the event that the publishers are contacted by any of the untraceable copyright holders after publication of this book, the publishers shall endeavor to rectify the position accordingly as soon as reasonably practicable.

The poems included in this collection have been reproduced by the kind permission of their authors, or are exempt from copyright, unless otherwise stated below.

"God"s Laughter" and "Poem From a Three Year Old" by Brendan Kennelly. Reproduced by permission of Bloodaxe.

"The Second Coming," "Never Give All the Heart," "The Fisherman," "What Then?" and "The Ballad of Father Gilligan" by W B Yeats. Reproduced with permission of AP Watt Ltd on behalf of Michael B Yeats.

"Father and Son" by F R Higgins. Reproduced by the kind permission of Ruth Dodd.

"The Rain Stick" and "Requiem for the Croppies" from *Opened Ground: Poems 1966–1996* by Seamus Heaney, published by Farrar, Strauss & Giroux. Reproduced with the permission of Farrar, Strauss & Giroux.

"Anseo" by Paul Muldoon from *Poems 1968–1998*, published by Faber and Faber. Reproduced with the permission of the author.

"Death of an Irishwoman" by Michael Hartnett. Reproduced by kind permission of the author and The Gallery Press, Loughcrew, Oldcastle, County Meath, Ireland, from *Collected Poems* (2000).

"Someone" by Dennis O'Driscoll from *Hidden Extras*, published by Anvil Press Poetry 1987. Reproduced with the permission of Anvil Press Poetry.

"Night Feed" by Eavan Boland. Reproduced with the permission of Carcanet Press Ltd.

"Bagpipe Music" and "The Sunlight on the Garden" by Louis MacNeice from *Collected Poems*, published by Faber & Faber. Reproduced by permission of David Higham Associates.

"Christy Brown Came to Town" by Richard Harris. Reproduced by permission of Noel Harris.

"Antarctica" and "Everything is Going To Be All Right" by Derek Mahon. Reproduced by kind permission of the author and The Gallery Press, Loughcrew, Oldcastle, County Meath, Ireland, from *Collected Poems* (1999).

"Thems Your Mammy's Pills" by Leland Bardwell. Reproduced by permission of The Dedalus Press.

"Ómós do John Millington Synge" by Máirtin Ó Direáin. Reproduced by permission of Stiofán Ó hAnnracháin.

"The Country Fiddler" by John Montague. Reproduced by kind permission of the author and The Gallery Press, Loughcrew, Oldcastle, County Meath, Ireland, from Collected Poems (1995).

"Solstice" by Gerry Dawe. Reproduced by kind permission of the author and The Gallery Press, Loughcrew, Oldcastle, County Meath, Ireland, from *The Lundy's Letter* (1985).

"The Boys of Barr na Sráide" by Sigerson Clifford. Copyright © The Estate of Sigerson Clifford 1986. Reprinted by permission of Mercier Press Ltd, Cork.

"Swineherd" by Eiléan Ní Chuilleanán. Reproduced by kind permission of the author and The Gallery Press, Loughcrew, Oldcastle, County Meath, Ireland, from *The Second Voyage* (1986).

"Peter Street" by Peter Sirr. Reproduced by kind permission of the author and The Gallery Press, Loughcrew, Oldcastle, County Meath, Ireland, from *Bring Everything* (2000).

"Plaisir D'Amour" by Patrick Galvin, reprinted by permission of Cork University Press.

"All of These People" from *The Weather in Japan* by Michael Longley, reprinted by permission of Random House UK.

"Pity the Islanders, Lucht an Oileáin" by David Quin, reprinted by permission of the author.

PHOTO CREDITS

Photos of Ireland © Getty Images
Patrick Bergin © Michael Tighe
Bono © Anton Corbijn
Pierce Brosnan © Greg Gorman
Gabriel Byrne © Roberto Dutesco
Liam Clancy – courtesy of Liam Clancy
Andrea Corr © Kevin Westenberg
Sharon Corr © Kevin Westenberg
Bill Cullen – courtesy of Bill Cullen
Danny Doyle © Robin Reid Photography
Ronnie Drew – courtesy of Ronnie Drew
Joe Duffy © RTÉ Stills Dept
Colin Farrell © AP/Wide World Photos
Marian Finucane – courtesy of Marian Finucane
Brenda Fricker – courtesy of Cassie Mayer Ltd
Gavin Friday © Mary Scanlon
James Galway © AP/Wide World Photos
Bob Geldof © Colm Henry
Brendan Gleeson – courtesy of Brendan Gleeson
Richard Harris © Colm Henry
Seamus Heaney © Norman MacBeath
Brendan Kennelly – courtesy of Brendan Kennelly
Pat Kenny – courtesy of Pat Kenny
Mick Lally © Joe O'Shaughnessy
John Lynch © Brian Moody
Ciaran MacMathuna – courtesy of Ciaran MacMathuna
Paddy Moloney © AP/Wide World Photos
Van Morrison © Paul Cox
Sinead O'Connor © AP/Wide World Photos
Daniel O'Donnell – courtesy of Daniel O'Donnell
Ardal O'Hanlon © David Schienmann
Micheal Ó Muircheartaigh © Kinane Studio
Milo O'Shea © James Shannon
Maureen Potter – courtesy of Maureen Potter
Jim Sheridan – Amelia Stein
Niall Toibin – Des Lacey
Bill Whelan © Colm Henry

ACKNOWLEDGMENTS

Special thanks to

Pat Balfe
Tom Barton
Suzie Bateman
John Bateson
Gordon Bolton
Jane Bolton
Pat Boran
Eimear Bradley
Amanda Brown
Richard Burke
Tony Byrne
Pierce Casey
Maurice Cassidy
Carol Coleman
Denise Conway
Amy Corrigan
Tom Costello
Deirdre Costello
John Cunningham
Noel Cusack
Jane Dalton
John Dardis
Anne Dargan
Denis Desmond
Liz Devlin
Theo Dorgan
Angela Douglas
Claire Doyle
Nigel Duke
Pat Dunne
Pat Egan
Ursula Fanning

Brian Farrell
Claudine Farrell
Rachel Fehily
Christine Fitzpatrick
Cyril Freaney
Barbara Galavan
Barry Gaster
Anita Gibney
Liam Giles
Justin Green
Brian Hand
Patricia Hanson
Jared Harris
Noel Harris
Shay Healy
Colin Henry
Caroline Hickson
Lindsay Holmes
Siobhan Hough
John Hughes
Ros and John Hubbard
Susan Hunter
Declan Jones
Helina Kearney
Steve Kenis
Brendan Kennelly
Peter Kenny
Joe King
Philip King
Kathy Kruse-Kennedy
David Landsman
Johnny Lappin

Paul Lenehan
Marty Miller
Eamon McCann
John McColgan
Alastair McGuckian
Cathal McLysaght
Yvonne McMahon
Avila Molloy
Mark Molloy
Nikki Molloy
Joe Moreau
Mike Murphy
Fiona Nagle
Bill O'Donovan
Fred O'Donovan
Dennis O'Driscoll
Jack O'Leary
Willie O'Reilly
Tom Owen
Lucia Proctor
John Redmond
Jean Reilly
Sara Ryan
John Sheehan
Dave Slevin
Norma Smurfit
Colin Stokes
Claire Strudwick
Joe Woods
Caitriona Ward
Paddy White
Philip Wood